Fate is everything. It is the past ... tain
point it comes to fruition, as he ... rking
her words through an ecstatic s) ... life of
the mind, mourning and celebrating who and what is lost as time goes
by. With her signature deftness she guides her lines directly into your
heart. You see and sing with them. Each right word takes your breath
away. "Saturation—the world is / its own music in awe and // space and
not flat these / dynamics of rising" "Two futures coincide"—the lucky
reader and this book. "Your somatics are your own" but, you will find, it
is your destiny to be enlightened by this *News*.

Laura Moriarty | *A Tonalist*

Early in these pages Norma Cole quotes Hafez as a warning to the
gentle reader—that in fact or in practice, *"under every deep / a lower deep
opens"*—and this book, this incredibly diagrammed advisory concerning
both "fate" and "news," plumbs startling depths and arrives at its final
moments with Ornette Coleman's question—"What do you expect?"—
and with Tassadit Yacine's approximation of Amrouche's uncomfortable
acceptance of Algerian identity—"I am the bridge." In between,
Norma Cole diagrams an astonishingly intricate map of power, the
"angel standing in the sun" that John mentioned in Revelations, and
how its loci are, again, in fact and practice wide-ranging. And, rife with
a homegrown ambiguity, the poems expand—grim Halloween turns up
twice like a bad penny, and the police turn up as well. But there's also a
luminous bar of elegies for Tom Raworth, Bill Berkson, Leslie Scalapino,
and David Bowie. ("Still Today" ends with a request or admonishment
for Bill Berkson: "So keep on / Proposing paradise.") And Norma Cole
instructs, "the world is / its own music in awe and // space and not flat."
Fellow gentle readers, *Fate News* is good news for all of us.

C.S. Giscombe | *Prairie Style*

Of all Norma Cole's collections, *Fate News* comes closest to the feeling of
being in the actual presence of the poet. It's as if the surface of her life is
laid out between the words and we are welcomed to ride, out beyond the
coast. "A meteor shower-constellation / as memory of perfection." This
form of rapture feels dependent on the grain and warp of chance. The
recurring dislocations are addictive and telling. Norma's line feels tuned
to the point of tremor, channeling and prophecy. "The anticipation
continuing the possibility of its / disruption." This collection also
contains "Ordinary Things" (for Tom Raworth), my favorite list poem
in recent years. Hold tight, this is the greatest glass box you will ever be
dropped into.

Cedar Sigo | *Royals*

Fate News

FATE NEWS

NORMA COLE

OMNIDAWN PUBLISHING
OAKLAND, CALIFORNIA
2018

Text set in Gill Sans Std & Garamond 3 LT Std

Cover and interior design by Sharon Zetter
Cover art by Stanley Whitney, Stay Song 11, 2017.
Image courtesy of the artist.

Offset printed in the United States
by Thomson-Shore, Dexter, Michigan
On 55# Enviro Natural 100% Recycled 100% PCW
Acid Free Archival Quality FSC Certified Paper

Library of Congress Cataloging-in-Publication Data

Names: Cole, Norma, author.
Title: Fate news / Norma Cole.
Description: Oakland, California : Omnidawn Publishing, 2018.
Identifiers: LCCN 2018014073 | ISBN 9781632430588 (pbk. : alk. paper)
Classification: LCC PR9199.3.C585 A6 2018 | DDC 811/.54--dc23
LC record available at https://lccn.loc.gov/2018014073

Published by Omnidawn Publishing, Oakland, California
www.omnidawn.com   (510) 237-5472   (800) 792-4957
10 9 8 7 6 5 4 3 2 1
ISBN: 978-1-63243-058-8

True revolution is an individual thing.

Antonin Artaud

For Care

TABLE OF CONTENTS

LOCAL

13

ONGOING

49

STAY SONGS FOR STANLEY WHITNEY

67

HARMOLODICS

75

L O C A L

Jupiter high & bright in the

Western night, signs &
Scars become shapes busy
Creating & destroying silent
Variables approaching the zero
Of dust and debris

And it was always drainage for angels
Gravity seen directly or heat loss
Miraged in the perfect orbit
Of fortune or the fiery

Great red spot & blurred
Bands of fire or its memory
Zones and binding threads, *angels*
Smoldering, red, ocher, yellow & white

AMONG THINGS

Aubade for David Ireland

what is
that chair
doing there?

resistance
"Come in!"
space between place

morning
ritual
motion

a feeling of expectation
"connecting fetish and compulsivity"
sounds of sanding, making, working

framing a set-up, just some
angels revealing a crack, repetitive
action references a carpet

of cement, a ball, alchemy
a "Broken Glass Repaired
by its Reflection"

*"under every deep
a lower deep opens"*
says Hafez

"the object allows
me to document
a thought"

"social relics"
cured with lime
travel to home

*

The Hassidim have a saying about the world to come. Everything there will be arranged just as it is with us. The room we have now will be just the same in the world to come…. Everything will be the same as here—only a little bit different. Thus it is with imagination. It merely draws a veil over the distance. Everything remains just as it is, but the veil flutters and everything changes imperceptibly beneath it. [Walter Benjamin, "In the Sun" 1932]

FOURTH OF JULY, 2015

For David Miller and Kevin Killian

At the Ice Cream Bar there were sweethearts and generations of parents, their grown children and grandchildren. "I'll have a butterscotch sundae," someone said.

He was far away now, but they were both thinking about the angel sitting at the top of the stele, on the wing of the golden angel.

It was a bookcase but opened like a door. It was a door. It was a *déjà-vu*.

If it had been a film, the handsome youth would have knelt down beside the old woman lying, then sitting, on the ramp, saying, "Are you all right?" Then, as she gingerly felt her right temple, he would have exclaimed, "You're bleeding! Do you want us to call an ambulance?" whereupon the old woman would have said "No," picked up her glasses, and stood up.

They rode on horseback through the jungle to the sea.

Fear of falling or fear of flying?

Local action, provisionally.

The tiny mice were scampering around the patio floor outside the café, then scurrying back to their nest under the wooden fence.

I listen to it over and over.

As her parents were getting their backpacks out of the trunk of the car, the little girl ran across the pavement and bent down over the spray of golden poppies.

A kiss like smoke flew from his lips.

Why the NO PARKING signs? There was no one working here. It was the fourth of July.

ASH NIGHT WOOD FOR CEDAR SIGO

Anything remembering night
After margins, sheets of last night
Birds, what remains after night
Comes, lighting the immune night
White sphinx under wood in the night

THE PAINTER'S MEASURE

For Nicole Phungrasamee Fein

Hope is encountered, variously
remembered, granted the patterns
of heaven—countless tiny
stars, oxalis hearts,
forget-me-nots, test sheets

Distant mountain ridgelines
flatten to paper in daylight
with every purposeful motion
night vision of timeless time
approaching the pulse of suspension

Metabolic edge of experiment,
the radiant points, scales and
variations of beads and dots
breathe benevolent notes, their
particular legibility of trackless

Resistance, deep-rooted, time
becomes sight incarnate, embodied
control framing chaos, space beyond
clarity, branches of lavender, thistle
grinding binding wetting the colors

A meteor shower—constellation
as memory of perfection

WHEN PUSH COMES TO SHOVE

Elegy for Leslie Scalapino

Nevermore is just a word
The crease of life
Rain's sweet scent or
The erasure of rain
Localized deafness—

As the wind folds other things
Go, go out and play
The nothing that stops
Time—check it

Fresh as rice powder
In the wind, perfect
Memento, remember
She lives

DISTRACTION

...a tendency toward silence
Paul Celan

When I was young, in Toronto, I used to listen to the radio, as I do now in San Francisco. There was a program the name of which I could not make out. Was it called "Maple Leaf Ballroom" or "Make Believe Ballroom"?

*

Waiting at the rehab, rereading the poem Cid Corman wrote for Anne-Marie Albiach. I read it on my phone, but if I had received it on paper in a letter, I would have brought it along.

*

but Jan, they're French cows...

*

Although someone had clearly been responsible for building the tiny park between warehouses on the bay, no one was looking after it now. Looked after or not, there were some young trees, a walkway, small rocks lining it. Even so, no end to Monarch butterflies twirling in pairs, white herons and gulls, and some other smaller shore birds walking or standing in the ebb and flow.

*

UBFRAGD on a license plate. The man ran with his dog, then put him back in the truck and drove away.

*

"My mother wanted me to become a doctor."
Boris Akunin, "Paradise Lost: Confessions of an Apostate Translator"
p.16, *TLS*, 2/15/13

*

My father thought I should play the harp, then "because of your French" I should be an interpreter at the UN. He thought I should be the person who at a party sits down at the piano and bangs out some tunes. We didn't have a piano when I was growing up so I didn't learn to play. Eventually my mother bought a used upright and put it in the basement under the stairs after having it painted grey.

*

invisible speech is not silence(d)

*

In those days, a few vans and trucks were still pulled by horses. One Saturday my father's friend was late. He was late to take me to Niagara Falls to see our cousins who lived there. He came into the house telling us that in the street a horse had reared up and came crashing down on the hood of his car, so we couldn't go to the Falls that day.

*

*

I don't know what those flowers are called so I'll just name their colors: red, mauve, orange.

BLACK FLOWERS

He said – long ago – that
myth was dead. He meant it.

"Myth is dead!"
"Long live myth!"

They are playing out
something. Legendary.

Picks up her glass. She
has a glass, with coffee,

ice and milk in it. Thinks
about the refugees on the

road. Road to what, to
where? With nothing but

their clothes on their backs.
Mythic and literal.

How to speak about them
and why? How to speak

to them. To keep them
in mind. In our minds.

"Bless you and keep you,"
so the prayer says.

NOWHERE POWER

Looks along the edge
of the sun

a signature of clouds
driftwood

to convey directly
through those texts

"I see an angel
standing in the sun."

...

"Nowhere do artists and writers have power, but nowhere in the world
do they have less power than in the United States."
Raúl Zurita (email correspondence, May 8, 2007, from Santiago, Chile
to Mexican poet Valerie Mejer)

I GOT WORD

I got word this morning that he died. Five days ago. I held back tears.
Why hold back, I thought. No one would even see. And if someone was
here to notice I could just explain. Explain what though? The "though"
is a bridge. To what end? I only met him once. We really met, I mean
had a preplanned meeting in a café on the rue Lagrange. The café was
probably called Café Lagrange. I chose it because it was familiar to me.
I'd been living around the corner on rue des Anglais, in the 5th
arrondissement, about which a friend living in the 9th said it did not
exist. He was driving, and told me with the certainty of a man living in
the 9th there was no such street. He—the man who had died five days
ago—I think he was wearing a V-neck sweater, cerulean blue. Or maybe
Bob was wearing that blue sweater when we first met at the Poetry
Center, his blond hair (I remember it as being blond) pulled back in a
ponytail. A tale, the long and short of it, was that I was crying for a man
I'd met once. When I saw him at the café—did he see me first or did I
see him first? I probably got there ahead of time and claimed the table.
I do that. I like to get there first, be there, as if I am always there at that
table in that café, have been there forever. He looked quite athletic, as
if he were a tennis player. Maybe he was a tennis player, had just come
from the courts. I can't remember whether or not he was carrying his
racquet. He looked very energetic for a writer. "Her hair, her hair," he
kept repeating, as though tossing his imaginary hair, as though berating
me for not being ravishing. I had long hair at the time but I knew by
his affect that he was not taken by my long hair. It was not luxuriant,
bewitching. She had beautiful thick hair, it was true, just look at the
one or two pictures that are around. He showed me the photos from an
old yellowed page of newsprint. It was from the TV section of an old
newspaper. Maybe it was just one photo. But I knew there must have
been more. That photographer snapping photos of the famous writer
that the man I was meeting had written a book about, and the not so
famous young poet with the fabulous hair, meeting in a café somewhere
in Paris or Berlin, must have developed the lot of them and given them
to the publisher, who paid him handsomely. Or to the editorial desk
who had chosen one image for the paper that probably had a slot for a
documentary about the famous writer. Where were the others? I had
tried to find out, had called the paper. That section didn't exist any

more. The person I spoke to said they didn't keep photos around. Why hadn't they archived them? When the famous writer that the man I was meeting had written a book about died, none of these images of him and the younger woman poet at a table in a café had come to light, so I knew they were telling the truth when they said they didn't have those photographs. The man who met me in the café to talk about the younger woman poet with bewitching hair said that they, they older, or younger, or middle-aged, or all of the above, the men talked among themselves about her hair. Did they whisper about it while she was walking past them on the street, or in a committee room when they got together to discuss their publishing projects? Did they talk about her fierce writing?

Pour Ludovic Janvier
Paris, 1934—20 janvier 2016

ODILE AND ODETTE WRITE BACK

To DLS

She gave us our names by looking
by thinking of a dance by wondering
what we were doing arms clasped

around each other's waist looking
through barbed wire looking up
through wire at the grandparents

looking down through wire at us.
Captured they couldn't come over
(Red Rover) stranded as we were

on different sides of the line. She
looked at this image of us and
wrote our names in ink.

ORDINARY THINGS

for Tom Raworth, from his poems

quill whales sail rig waves crowns hum sound body chips hythe
saxophone faces earshot ration leaves moments deck potatoes animal
memoirs kindling roses tulips lily oyster leg history panther
chimneys sheep red lentils monkey granite amber pennies eyes threads
shit tin tomato meat time liquid song tag hailstones nemesis nation
mist lemon sill moist philosophies bosom midnight horizon flames
wind toy voyage chemicals bubble orange smoke embers beach tunics
splendour mushroom night tip state organs worker worlds store
swan dream dark porch gravel universe curtain thought coffin miner
method tension surface breeze coast apples ashes crew home news food
yellow bag days rhythm bomb paper heroin brain maggots love
lightning stanzas smile submarine summer gale questions couch
alcohol playground boy hole devil label wires ink orchard rim work
gangways glitz skin gesture armour band mercury wheel clothes walls
experiences boxes gas balloon hair belt wreckage empire valves
weeds germ ice-cream root tune oils window stairs stars moon
disguise place object pavement flesh strategy women children lorries
train clock sites sleep pasture ground animal shelter heart years body
drops country forest tissues green fruit food basket eyelids fabric
pebbles machines power blood war nature wood snow glass bird
feather   footstep   exit   sky   library   book   name   vision

STILL TODAY

for Bill Berkson

It's still today
Be still

Is it far where you are?
Beyond the furthermores and the afterwards

Sway me now
Notice the hook

Or failed star
Or jailed target

The force of it
User interface blindsided

Or neurological space
It has a logic to it, you could

Force an elegy: social practice
The war, the cold river water

Formation, disruption, the lamp
Suddenly begins to flicker

So keep on
Proposing paradise

PASTORAL

pour Melissa, Femme de Belleville

You, Belleville Bee, born in the bountiful region of New Jersey, of
the magnolia, the flowering dogwood, horse chestnut and
crab apple, paulownia and lilac, rhododendron and Carolina silver bells,
of the Tiger Woods and the Lauryn Hill

of the space race and the cold war, the wood rabbit,
Watergate and the Fall of Saigon, rejoice! Sing sweetly, all ye warblers,
goldfinches and nuthatches, ruby-throated hummingbirds,
thrushes and thrashes and dark-eyed juncos!

This is just to say in *The Land That Time Forgot*, in the year 1975, along
with the first episode of SNL, *Jaws*, *Shampoo*, The Wheel of Fortune,
the Weather Underground and Angelina Jolie, it was a Saturday on the
sixth day in the merrie month of May

when you first appeared: *Joyeux anniversaire*!

SKY WAVE FOR REX RAY

*One can climb a beanstalk up into heaven
and see how angels make gold.*
Ernst Bloch

Colors play on a whim in a teardrop realm freestyle *the spiders from Mars*
or is that your shadow?

I LOVE BEAUTY!

Silver and blue diamonds, pink and yellow gingham, kinetic tension the
magic of the unseen acrobat, skydiver, high wire artist

Constructing freehand rockets, arcs, a string of pearls, those parabolic
flowers, sails and waves, whiskers, nets, sets of them *in the dance hall*

I LOVE BEAUTY!

Dreamlike and razor sharp ritual of scissors, paper and glue, uncanny *in
a most peculiar way* just like those cool white ankle boots timeless in their
timeliness

Oil and water, trial and error, the calculated crystalline hard-edged mys-
tery of art & design "I live on that line"

Tone on tone, saturated "just put the colors next to each other and they
find a way to work"

A party when it's dark *this serious moonlight* scent of pot reverie and the
unexpected like Skeeter "a sign from the universe"

Close to you, moondust shimmers in red and pink on purple, textures and
patterns *on a roll* left *ground control* behind

I LOVE BEAUTY!

Starlight in your eyes stealing show after show, as you left the building you called WE ARE ALL MADE OF LIGHT

YOU SING AND THE ANGELS SMILE

for Alex Katz

You could have
heard a pin drop

and then the burnished
trumpets singing to

the choir, the hierarchy
of the Angels, the Cherubim

with six wings and four
heads, the Seraphim, Archangels

Michael, Gabriel, Raphael
et al. writing code up there

in Heaven, the Powers and the
true Angels brushing against us

the Virtues, spirits of motion
controlling the elements

the "shining ones" governing
the seasons, the stars and the moon

in charge of miracles, providing
courage, grace and valor

wings of desire unseen and unheard
so faraway, so close and then

the fallen ones, Zepar who makes
women love men, Vepar appears

as a mermaid and Vassago discovering
lost and hidden things.

The Angels with Mary and Destiny
and all the ladies in the paintings.

BLM

Soon it will
be Halloween again
and we'll all
put on our
masks or
some other
chokehold

The man was kissing the other man near the ladder or he was whisper-
ing in his ear, or to his ear.
On a wall was painted the question "Have you tasted all my flavors?"
"All my flavors" was in the same script as "Have you tasted," just a lot bigger.
On the pavement outside the convenience store a woman was lying on
her side, asleep, a brown blanket over the upper half of her torso.

Surface tension
masked as
insolence
intentional action
stripped naked
clear temper
"please just leave me alone"

If you come across an unconscious person take out your weapon. Fire
your weapon.
At a swimming pool, if you come across a girl in a bathing suit, push
her to the ground. Throw your back into it. Shove your knee on her
back. Take out your weapon.

MOUNT FIASCO

The young woman in her
sparkly dress, looking out
from the bridge of
sighs or the glassed-in
counter of a café

I heard the mortars again
tonight

forbidden to interfere

looks at his timepiece again

time or what?

need help? hell no he says, it's
the same angel

CLOCK

        SKIP   SEL which in French
                              means salt

LOT FULL

every night
stung by light

            essays
            he says

        turning the page
        naming it

glass on fire
a circle of smoke

SYLLABARY OF A SIMPLE TEXT

I thought of language.
Layli Long Soldier

That the white woolly dog on the steps could speak
was not the surprise, but that he spoke Inuit

for instance, softly falling snow, snow good for driving
sled, wet snow that can be used to ice a sleigh's runners

crystalline powder snow that looks like salt, snow shaped
in tongues blown by the wind, crunchy snow, refrozen snow

snow in eye, melting snow, divination in snow
eternal snow north of the tree line

east winds are strong and bring bad weather, 2:45 pm
dusk in Iqaluit, a baby in the hood of her parka

ideas come through an instrument, a V on her forehead
the colors, how they sound, singing darkness, then

brightness into the cello, splicing the exhalation
which makes a dark growling barking with

inhalation, the higher notes, a trilling
inhale sharply: the current sheet becomes

wavy when the sun's magnetic field begins
to flip out to the heliosphere

the elders say the axis has shifted
heavy metals or mortals gesticulating

geomagnetic reversal seems to be happening
sooner, the pole moving toward Siberia

where the Cyrillic alphabet is used to translate
transliterate from Inuktitut

The dog said in translation, "The theoretical
antidote is not working."

The house was a square block of concrete, snow
all around. Red block letters on the concrete face

above and beside the door said THEORETICAL
ANTIDOTE

* * *

Like that smaller sea
hemmed in by land

the floor was slippery
made of ice

sometimes I would have that dream
Arctic Gold and Exploration Syndicate

we played with dolls
his eye fell out

the ice was shifting
aiyaya sing

* * *

face to face, we held
each other's arms

* * *

foxes turn white

tiny snowblind stitches a watertight
parka made of skins of birds

"We don't believe. We fear"
and watch the shoreline

R.I.P JEFFREY CLYDE WILKES

We are all children of the earth, and, at some time,
she will take us back to herself again.
Thich Nhat Hanh

Harsh, bitter, sad occasion mars
And marks last Saturday

The day you died. By those pure eyes
I have to do this, she said

You are a part of us, she said
Like the fragrance of the North Carolina

Magnolia, with its leaves of green
And silver, its ivory flowers

And like hickory, in spring
With its green and yellow catkins

Or weeping autumn juniper with
A red-shouldered hawk soaring

Above Gaston County. On that Saturday
There was a sighting

Of the white ibis, robins, chickadees
Hummingbirds, warblers, wrens

And song sparrows.

PARDON ME

It jumps through the window,
kneels on the table
Marosa di Giorgio

1.
The pardon is on the table. What pardon? What table? I'll pardon
myself. Pardon me. The pardon, what does it look like? Its dimensions?
Can we see it? Can we taste it? Ah. We smell it. I remember. Do you?
Rife with pardons. Green pardons. Misty-blue pardons. Silver, gold and
crystal pardons. Denim pardons, corduroy pardons, silk purse for a sow's
pardons, velvet pardons.

2.
Decaf of pardons
Great Barrier Reef of pardons
Great Depression of pardons
Fluke of pardons

Why say "so nice
and quiet" when it
was so nice and
quiet? My err

WIZORD SAYZ RONG WERK

Fieldwork of pardons
Common dragonflies of pardon
Uncommon dragonflies of pardon
Buchenwald of pardons

What to do with all those dead ends?

HALLOWEEN 2

For Joanne Kyger

Holy Cow! Hope the

Jack O'Lantern doesn't

run for president

is what we're

all thinking

these days

#3

for Laura Moriarty

if or when one of the magical seals
gives way when does the first parade
of theories begin bracing myself
to outside worked up bright bands
beside normal a problem of tapes then
a record of events
overhauling nostalgic to long ago
pushing a flood of tears in its
slightly elliptical orbit
evidently referring to what I must have
ceased to be in order to be *who* I am
and the iron moon of Jupiter to imagine
the veins the grooves and ridges of ice
the night sidereal Io's volcanoes
fit into a box, even where the sky
was my own, but every question
painted ultramarine

She can't see that far

absence of sign means sign

the emptying out

a ring of smoke

the missing act

this is it, and this too

marking time, eternity is useless

19 June, 2017

ONGOING

Along the moraine in the Carolinian forest
maples had already begun to turn red

in those days people wrote memory
in books not sticks, singing sometimes

I live in the country, sometimes
I live in town or in a dream

like state, that's tiger to you, a big
heat wave, many days remaining

until the end of this year, walking
the land, summer grass and spadesful

of earth, a rectangle, sun on it
just that

It's just that

peridot is

your birthstone

but your

mystical Tibetan

birthstone dating

back over

a thousand

years is

diamond

ἀδάμας

unbreakable

diamond

cuts through

illusion, atoms

strong covalent bonding

no form

no fear

magma, eruption

compassion

And on that day

from your window

the steel heart

red ratchet and pawl

a fixed arc

chained to the hoist of

the working arm

horizontal jib

on the mast

in the sky

By far

the best

magnolias

seen through a

screen, so many

lasting

so long

carpels tough as nails

surviving ice ages

continental drift

Saffron

rose mallow

worn behind your

left ear

changing and preserving

wrapped in tiger skin

demon slayer

holds its color

even in the hottest

summer days

Sun in rips and starts

ascending ragas

for rippling

winnowing

retting

scutching

heckling

spinning sasheen

to wrap

and swaddle

Woven moonlight

pulled by hand from earth

linen from line

or Nile where

flax grew

exceedingly soft threads

irregular shapes

peculiar as tigers' patterns

no two stripes alike

Hydrangea

blooms perseverance

breathing unfurling

a block print tiger

alert, incised

by a table

near a drum

on a carpet

revived from

the sealed cave

in Dunhuang

Fine-grained, watertight

catkins, wings, heart-shaped

leaves, silver shadow

will ignite from

the smallest spark

branches rest

during the night

birch bark fragments

found at the site

Did you plant

the ivory silk

lilac, its broad

panicles appearing

in early summer

its bark like

black cherry and

like the wolf willow

part of the olive

family tree?

Two

white-tailed deer

a large brown

moth, a cicada

shedding its skin

the impossibility

of repetition

of one

water lily

on the Credit River

Descending ostinato

in the seventh movement

glass harmonica

cues for the entrance

of a private

performance

morning ascending

catches on the figure of

a feather on an old t-shirt

a city

named for a reed

Tiger runs wild

waning crescent

28% or 29% visible

not many images

illuminated crescent edge

casts long shadows

seen from earth, the moon

getting closer to the sun

can't be directed

Tumulus

barrow

kurgan

mound, bank

kneeling and arranging

tugging on your breath

hazel poles or stakes

no hill overlooking

the sea, placeholder

filled with treasure

STAY SONGS

FOR STANLEY WHITNEY

1

Saturation – the world is
its own music in awe and

space and not flat these
dynamics of rising

horizon remember the narrow
loom's scale, perspectival

innuendo's subtle registration
of touch, we listen, eye

in the hand, mind
in the eye of the hand

2

Rhythmic animation, shapes
shimmer continents:

fullness of measure
of range, vibrato opening onto

attention's staccato conditions:
harmonics of time, of tone of

mind in time of emotion
in mind of emotion, philology

of paint, resistance, the retinal
surface is paint the working

space where experience,
mysterious, takes place

3

Motion captures color
its own musical dream
of salt water and fresh
water

colors that
fall, that slow-drag
an asymmetrical
time line, lost

and found structure
emerging from these
tonal relational
painted facts

4

This way
world is
point of
departure, painter's
attention in
time for
the work.

Resolutions need
space, open
presence, take
place.

5

There will be
time
then
there will be
song

for the paintings
say
stay

HARMOLODICS

What do you expect?
Ornette Coleman

SUDDENLY HESITANCIES QUIETNESS

There are those who pronounce *flaneur* to rhyme with *sewer*, something like a placeholder, ecstatic to discover Hearing held the window, the river, like *that* producing one Day as another "rival publication" *that* for One, *there* another dictionary beyond "affinity"

the burden of the Moon was surprising and ambitious presence of the super natural world Remembers the dream where initials of the character-object were Those of a different poet kept in mind for very different Reasons

Turbulent tonight, contact and context "singing in the spirit" Fills in from sight to mind, painters seriously silent making a Horoscope he will say time is tax we will say time is free she will say time Time out

what does anything reveal "by virtue of its structure" the Frequency of the word Secret in these accounts there was a door Here once the opening of the—wound? exhaust deeply hidden in trying to separate the sensory

statement is as statement does Resist repeating on paper, its yellow edge enriched by relief of the victim by the role of the suffering victim Suddenly her voice a phrase precise Hesitancies from sight to mind

written in water Through the window of a book, the ultimate Quietness of its ending—not ending in the empty room

EAT THE BEANS

Now eating the beans is much like eating the parents' heads.
Plutarch, *Moralia*

The rolling thing is:
the poem is expected to return home
to return to the tonic, as a child

And as a musician I say to you:
a series of substitutions, "it's
my turn to talk now"

I offer this object in:
disguise as food a color
in disguise as a lover

Saint A is forever holding:
out his flaming head
I take your words into my mouth

I am an arrival and a city in which order is not yet established:
in which order has not yet been erased I eat the seat of order

A musician's:
liver is a man's heart
on a certain street
Suddenly this tale meets: the naked violinist, back
to the window as she practices
The impulse to disrupt:
the reading continuously
by some any short version

A vision of expansion:
so they'll post the card
keep it—I am sent

"LOOK FOR THAT MAN IN THE MOON."

Hesitancies. A dog discovers its
color, its source. From sight
to mind without the dream in
which initials
of time

Don't eat the heart.
                              Pythagoras

                    There we were having
        on the spot
Lunch *on the grass* at the site

                "as you May know"
and
                "in the new year"

Do you like the feeling of
what happens in the *chamber*
                in the song? limitation
stains as a lover

the second shelf second
guessing no long
time project – *missing*

Grass stains – *is it an argument that builds?* –
Don't eat that

                          You really
Thought about it
not for long

A person's name means
          I-don't-know
Because of the coming of
          those letters
          another volume called
          outcast variables
          (how do you know which is
          which?) in the form of the
          night watchman's

logic of dismemberment
variously penned in wings

ALBA

People make rules at dawn

people shaped damp of work, purple
cord, brown tile, white tape
shadow, the room smells
like fuel like exhaust

[UCHRONIA ("memory under construction")]

People make rules called fundamental

THE NIGHT WATCHMAN

full of promise

she lives it

the object hove to
the instrument serves to reinforce
the sound of the voice

"à quoi?" [de Musset] she dreams

upon silent words

He hated hearing last things. It was the breath, the quantity of oxygen in the blood. The rhetoric of the blood. It presents itself directly to the senses.

LITA'S CHROMATICS

SF Newark

repeat: breach of form breeds form

muscle beyond apprehension

"do you have a problem with my knitting?"

"how the rock's asshole" is a phrase, a move, a police procedural, right Ben?

The hero comes to grief, grief leads to the beheading, the face of a cat, loss of face, a collision "and all the missing parts."

After all, the saint missed the dragon's heart. But who will be the saint? And later runs the risk of suddenly remembering who it was that had signed, the recipient, thanks and other references.

No one has slept on her belly in front of that fire, her closed eyes, face turned aside. A letter becomes a coincidence "the contemporary" steps on a plastic cup. Those whose house it was are supporting characters, imports heroes. They think it's theirs because they perceive it. Beauty works intermittently. The last word never ends, they still love.

He comes back, he will have been right, he does not, he will have been wrong. I think that's why, right Jack? or think that's right. You want it to be as real as this page, placing the photograph face down on the floor under the chair, the blue turn of conscience resolving in the center.

Your somatics are your own.

[INDIAN STORE ON 5TH]

metal arrow on a wooden base
heart-shaped fracture, atoms of color, dancing
unaccountability wanted to say how he piled hot coals on top
unfolding in the form of a joke going back decades and just like that she
was gone and just like that they having given up

cut up, they're not acting, this could be a good thing, first line
like sugar cookies, fancy sugar cookie procedures: the man in the shirt
dissolved the assembly, not for the first time, against all odds against
gravity *et tout*

The decision to start squaring off, start a new page, on to the
top, moving the population around, this story or the old story? This
story is the old story.

all the ones with ties
within seconds
while some of the victims' children watched. Don't mention it.
"It is raining on the city." [Feraoun, *Journal*, 1 Nov. 1955]
The pencil slides down.
He did not like have anything to say to me. The idea remained.
The idea remains an idea, go through my changes proliferate
She saves them, folds for a rainy day. The impulse to carry them
one at a time, place them. She took the photo, looked at his face, kissed
it and placed it carefully where no one could see it.

"DON'T WAIT TOO LATE." [EDDY MCCOY]

moving day

indigo

ratio: the anger of fear is to the anger of grief :: the anger of grief is to the fear of anger

required a dream of light or time gets saved up there in the negative space there in the still life

and the body of the clock called context

or bridge

"I am the bridge." [Tassadit Yacine]

a floating document, a listening document called the era of asymmetrical wingspan in an unnatural position

hung in the upper window

through-composed, the word for phantoms of the beloved becomes the word for imagination

How'd the living be reviewed by the dead?

talking together, head on upside-down

"Hold your breath and think of Spinoza." [Erwin Wurm]

understand the impulse to sing in the cellar, street named after them now and an empty desk mindful of a double life, the enemy living as the other

relationships are similar, not the things, their interruptions "what is zinc anyway?" or "to the person who knows me best" the quietness of the story or its lack of ending, not lacking not ending

knitting together at a different remove, a fruitful misunderstanding

and the painters seriously silent in the choppy air, surprise as expected

And if people can't see it, discursive, the burden of the moon, love or thanks, if the role fits, hesitancies as well as working on their own, the piper is resting, see him, resisting

A real life desire for bad medicine, a breath constellation, the metal needle jumping, a little performance as a million irrelevant questions to no end but to file in the form of a performance

formance: the sentence of the music

extremities: murder, gesture, missed sympathies

imagined the smell of the sea
impasses and obstacles, inklings

SO WHAT ABOUT ASSUMPTION OF REPETITION

Ascent intact

Two futures coincide

A tension accumulates between the rhythm as it is experienced
and the expectation of its fulfillment, the anticipation
Continuing the possibility of its
Disruption

A plate of corn offered a kind of organization as if a door behind
the podium, luxury, distortion, risk

and now for the revenge fantasy:
        "He could have shouted, and he could not" [Beckett]

But, but, but
the clouds are moving

WE SHOULD BE ABLE TO SEE

By this paint
populous music falls best steady
progression at different angles
beat from the whole not from the part
image cool as thought
steady changing beat and changing
falling spectral petals

LEAKING'S A CAPITAL SIN

handcrafted by father and
son, point of no
return, My Old Flame
a green tin trunk
doing the bunnyhop to
separate spoken kicks in
universal time

THE SUN

and the faint sun paradox, the asteroid behind you, return of
the Dumbbell Nebula, the Cloud Factory, Eagle, Triffid and Harpsi-
chord

Theories, Orion, imagine awakening with a flower in your hand
and not recognizing it

You long for familiarity and for the strangeness of the moon,
the dirty snowballs
And along came that cosmic timeline, crystal, from snow,
inside a crystal dolphin from Carthage, minerals float, their daughter,
square with the head of spring, signed by the glassblower, Jason of
Greece

A boy, or a little boy in a bear suit, desire on his tongue, affec-
tion, steep steps, escape valve, safety?
Being driven to safety as the sense of being kidnapped and
dragged into someone else's design
Is the subject still nothing
The danger lived next door posing as a bed of roses or clean-up
guys

ASSUMPTION, RECEPTION, CORRUPTION

"It is entirely characteristic..."
ideology is no excuse
too bad you can't see it, obscured as it is in memory
the kite of argument, now you see it
called away by life, a red letter day variously penned in wings
one didn't understand why were they dancing? He understood nothing
about the dancing. Ribbed ritual vertical
"let's talk about fish," he'd said, elbows leaning on the bed at
dawn at the side of the bed a person refuses conditions chooses "tennis
anyone" coming at it from far around potholes, toilets, lock-down

ineptitude

that glove

WASTE

In terms it is setting for itself. It should all be easily under-
stood.

HOW?

(to identify? To increase our shared

pulse of resistance: the decisive moment: long line of resistance
or "working space" [Stella]
in front, a whole paragraph with no skin just lying there bleed-
ing under shirts partly torn away

CONTINGENT TANGENT

The table was glass like the sea, things
Floated, shocked, frozen, little
Warships and such
An hour later his heart gave way

Lita arrived early, shocked to see your
Talking a large view winter presentation of the
Body separated only by land and
Desire, distance, wavelength, blood, rain

Testimony, documentary, distinctiveness
Admitting of an uncertain and indeterminate
Something to think about something
Someone cooked up "Because the deepest

Revolution is not social" [Will Alexander]

SECOND ALBA

*"...a gang of five, from whom I took
the mirror of gesture."*

Puzzle:
the part that's coming back

Or the point at which they no longer recognize each other singing
weeping into the breach. But when they meet on the plateau,

        item: tossing branches,
        horses, lions' manes,

the adjective is absorbed into the whitening of the sky

Lita stood in the snow, a photograph not taken [in her red scarf,
coat, boots, in mid-step] the elements, the elements, aorta
is how we'd translate that scream in the physically discontinu-
ous space (can you imagine any other?)
"It's the beefcake that kept you awake."
The seam was in your mind, air really.

SUGAR WINGS

I'd have been able to find your keyhole with my eyes shut.
Jean-Paul Sartre, *The Flies*

flies sing love songs
there are secret rhythms in their
love songs. Some flies
are unlucky in love

the rhetoric of flies is
the pulse

This one, then, in good time. Madge leaves the Leland Hotel, a pebble
and a penny on the sill, fate map referring to the building in the music,
not trying to reproduce it.

overtones, elegy, *that*
high voice past
the midpoint.

"my free will has a
mind of its own"

"straight trade,"
Lita wrote, tugging on events, a two-ton weight on her line. The house
is gone, the hotel is gone. Madge, that is not your

brother
in the photograph

KEEP. PLAYING. KID.

Lita is equal
to the world, in
that they both
are of a certain
age. A kind of
            continuous
scansion, imprudence

brings it back from the air

VIRIDIAN

The frame building before the stores went up, about holding back, "I completely want to hear this" tiny scarab above her left eye in my country, the reed of translation, moving, approaching, said, saying

       brimstone, saltpeter and amber, two
    signatures, one above the other, a bribe, do you ever
    get angry at me when I say no? Yes. Then I'm doing my job

in splendid isolation understood as someone's mourning, marble and rice, beeswax, milk and wood, found in the street, made on the spot, marking time, his beaded tenor sound

LIKE A FISH IN A DUMPSTER

    Any further controversy would figure, figure hummingbirds in
Manhattan then Charlie Parker
      synapsoids
beyond function when eyeless eyes are smiling watching you in my sleep
Should we show the exchange of papers? Was it
      successful?
Too soon to see the facets, their moving images surprise the other two
upon which were beings, projected time
      included – walked over
clap if you want by the new moon which causes things to grow long and
thin, while the full moon causes growth that is short and
        wide
Mercy does not come from the sky

ACKNOWLEDGMENTS

Unititled ("Jupiter high & bright") Commissioned broadside, 2nd floor projects 2017.

"Among Things: Aubade for David Ireland" Commissioned for catalog for *David Ireland*, San Francisco Art Institute 2016.

"ASH Night Wood for Cedar Sigo" Commissioned for *Bronze Chimes: Poems after Alfred Starr Hamilton*, Frank Haines 2017.

"The Painter's Measure" Commissioned for the catalog *Haunted Formalism*, works by Nicole Phungrasamee Fein and Dean Smith, 2016, presented by VOLUME at Del Vaz Projects.

"Distraction" *Touch the Donkey*, Issue One 2014.

"Black Flowers" Commissioned by *eye magazine*, photographs by Dennis Letbetter, Volume 9, 2016. Audio at https://www.poetryfoundation.org/features/audio/detail/89609

"Nowhere Power" *Best American Experimental Writing*, Wesleyan University Press 2018.

"I Got Word" *Touch the Donkey*, Issue Eleven 2016.

"Odile and Odette Write Back" *women : poetry : migration: {an anthology}*, Theenk Books 2017.

"Ordinary Things" Tom Raworth issue of *Critical Quarterly* 2017.

Bill Berkson Memorial, San Francisco Art Institute, 2016. *The Canary Island Connection: 60 Contemporary American Poets*, Zasterle Press 2016.

"Pastoral" Commissioned by Brent Cunningham for Melissa Benham's birthday 2015.

"Sky Wave for Rex Ray" Commissioned by Gallery 16 for *REX RAY:*

WE ARE ALL MADE OF LIGHT 2017.

"You Sing and the Angels Smile" Commissioned for *You Smile and the Angels Sing*, etchings by Alex Katz 2017.

"R.I.P. Jeffery Clyde Wilkes" Commissioned for Jeffrey Clyde Wilkes of Gaston County, North Carolina, August 8, 2015, for LAMENT FOR THE DEAD, an online community poetry project marking the death of every person killed by police and every police officer who loses life in the line of duty in the summer of 2015.

"Pardon Me" *GRAMMA* 2018.

"Halloween 2" Broadside, Omnidawn 2018.

"ONGOING" *Posit: A journal of literature and art* 2018,
      https://positjournal.com/

"STAY SONGS FOR STANLEY WHITNEY" Commissioned for Bill Maynes Gallery catalog 2001.

An earlier version of "HARMOLODICS" (titled "Coleman Hawkins Ornette Coleman") appeared as a chapbook from Horse Less Press 2012.

"Sudden Hesitancies Quietness," "Eat the beans," "Untitled (There we were . . .)," "Don't Wait too Late" *Hambone 16*, Fall 2002

Thanks to all the editors and publishers.

Once again, thank you Stanley Whitney for "cover art."

Thanks to Rusty Morrison, Ken Kegan and the team at Omnidawn.

This book is dedicated to Carolyn Zeifman Cronenberg.

NORMA COLE is a poet, translator and visual artist. Her books of poetry include *Actualities* (Litmus Press), *Where Shadows Will: Selected Poems 1988—2008* (City Lights), *Win These Poster and Other Unrelated Prizes Inside* (Omnidawn) and *Spinoza in Her Youth* (Omnidawn). *TO BE AT MUSIC: Essays & Talks* appeared in 2010 from Omnidawn. Her translations from the French include Danielle Collobert's *It Then* (O Books), *Crosscut Universe: Writing on Writing from France* (Burning Deck), and Jean Daive's *White Decimal* (Omnidawn). She has work in anthologies such as *Resist Much / Obey Little*, *American Hybrid: a Norton Anthology of New Poetry*, *Best American Experimental Writing*, and *women: poetry: migration {an anthology}*. Cole has had poems in many magazines and journals including *Gramma*, *Posit*, *Art in America*, *Bomb*, *Hambone*, *Sulfur*, *Conjunctions*, *HOW2*, *Talisman* and *Acts*. Her visual work has been shown at 2nd floor projects, California Historical Society and New College of California, and is included in the exhibition "Way Bay" at the Berkeley Art Museum. Born in Toronto, Canada, Cole has lived and worked in the sanctuary city of San Francisco for the past 40 years.

Fate News
by Norma Cole

Cover art by Stanley Whitney, Stay Song 11, 2017.
Image courtesy of the artist.

Text set in Gill Sans Std and Garamond 3 LT
Cover and interior design by Sharon Zetter

Offset printed in the United States
by Thomson-Shore, Dexter, Michigan
On 55# Enviro Natural 100% Recycled 100% PCW
Acid Free Archival Quality FSC Certified Paper

Publication of this book was made possible in part by gifts from:
Mary Mackey
Francesca Bell
Katherine & John Gravendyk, in honor of Hillary Gravendyk
The Clorox Company
The New Place Fund

Omnidawn Publishing
Oakland, California
2018

Rusty Morrison & Ken Keegan, senior editors & co-publishers
Gillian Olivia Blythe Hamel, senior poetry editor & editor, *OmniVerse*
Trisha Peck, managing editor & program director
Cassandra Smith, poetry editor & book designer
Sharon Zetter, poetry editor, book designer & development officer
Liza Flum, poetry editor
Avren Keating, poetry editor & fiction editor
Anna Morrison, marketing assistant
Juliana Paslay, fiction editor
Gail Aronson, fiction editor
SD Sumner, copyeditor
Emily Alexander, marketing assistant
Terry A. Taplin, marketing assistant
Matthew Bowie, marketing assistant
Mia Raquel, marketing assistant